From one parent to another…

Welcome to

The
Gluten-Free Parent's
Survival Guide

5 Steps to Helping Your
Gluten-Free Child
***THRIVE** in Every Way*

By Elyn JOY
"The Gluten-Free Parent"

2ⁿᵈ Edition
Now with
even more
indispensable
tips, advice, &
professional
input!

…bringing the best of what we've learned to you to help ease
your transition. Remember, you are not alone!

The Gluten-Free Parent
glutenfreeparent.com / Denver, Colorado USA

©2019 *To Tell the World Publishing,* Denver, Colorado

The Gluten-Free Parent's Survival Guide
2nd Edition

U.S. Library of Congress (LCCN)
by **The Gluten-Free Parent ™**
and
©To Tell the World Publishing

To Tell The World

Printed in the United States of America
Distributed in the US, Canada, and Worldwide

Dill Pickles

2 cups Kosher coarse salt)add to 9 qt
2 cups white vinegar   ) cold water
garlic-pulverized
pickling spices
fresh dill

In each quart jar;
fill with cucumbers
1 teaspoon picking spices(take/hot red hots)
1 teaspoon garlic   out
fresh dill (use plenty)
add water mixture; not used for 24 hours;
                                    tighten jar

put on lid lightly;
add more liquid mixture;

For Mom...

Wherever you are,
Debi, Eliot, and I know you are
cooking or baking up something wonderful!

Table of Contents

Before we begin...

Prepare for Everything
—and Nothing—
to Change

Dear Friend,

*I'm Elyn Joy, the Gluten-Free Parent. And yes, even though that may be my name in this book and in some of my work, I fully realize that the correct term is "**a**" gluten-free parent. I am **a gluten-free parent**, just like you. With this handbook, you have arrived at a place of safety, encouragement, and immense understanding.*

Elyn Joy, the *Gluten-Free Parent*, and daughter Edyth

Before we begin, let me tell you how I got here, and why I believe I am someone who can help you — both through the transition of becoming a gluten-free parent, and beyond that point towards your child's healthy, happy, and well-adjusted future as a gluten-free citizen of any community.

As an author and career educator, I've come to realize that knowledge alone does not equate to understanding. Rather, to understand something fully, we must go beyond facts and statistics and really grapple with the material — face it directly, exchange energy with it, and sometimes (by choice or not) LIVE it. It's through such interaction that things become real to us.

So how does this apply to our subject at hand? Well, when our daughter Edyth was first tested for celiac disease, it wasn't because she showed any major symptoms. True, her slowed growth and frequent headaches eventually pointed the way, but there was something else — an intuition, a gut feeling, an understanding of our daughter — that led us to insist on having her doctor investigate. The same went for the diagnosis of celiac.

> Knowledge without understanding and experience is like a flower without color or fragrance.
> – T. Hameed

It wasn't enough to merely read the jumble of sources handed over by doctors. The websites describing the medical aspects of this disease, the forums, the recipe sites — each had something to offer, but each held only a small fragment of the puzzle. It took weeks and months and years to understand what this all meant and how it would manifest in our lives as a family.

My father-in-law, a gastroenterologist in Tucson, spent hours on the phone with me on many occasions, fielding my questions and sharing news on research, new methods, and the repercussions of this new life. I joined the Gluten Intolerance Society and the National Celiac Association and became a certified Gluten-Free Safe Choices Provider. Still, however deep my personal quest for knowledge went, it couldn't touch the subtler lessons that just had to be lived and learned in the years that followed.

It didn't teach me how to deal with the tears after a lunchtime of teasing or the sadness of having to turn down a gingerbread-building experience (later, we learned that wearing gloves or washing hands right away would have made it okay). All the knowledge harvested in greedy bounty proved fruitless when I felt helpless, or heartbroken, or alone at the immensity of the changes in my daughter's (and our) life. Those things required a different kind of strength—more of the kind that comes naturally to superheroes or characters in fairy tales. It took bravery and heart and a great welling of optimism to find the way.

*So, since my mother was a locally famous cook and baker (she's also the inspiration for my forthcoming cookbook, **Dorothy's Kitchen**), I brushed myself off and jumped into gear, starting with safety measures and moving straight to the kitchen. I schooled myself via gluten-free cookbooks and websites and eventually graduated to transforming pretty much any recipe into gluten-free (thereby no longer relying on specified cookbooks!). I strongly recommend you do the same—or at least learn the basics and even a bit beyond, as outlined in Step 5 of this book.*

Volunteering at my daughter's school further illuminated the need for self-advocacy in any gluten-free child. It also underscored the challenges faced by allergy-prone kids in general, even as the world comes around to this increasingly common reality. There, I learned how to help educators by raising awareness and mindfulness around the world of class parties, field trips, and peer pressure. Above all, I committed each day to creating a safe and inspiring home, one wherein our daughter could truly thrive not just physically, but intellectually and emotionally as well. In that sense and beyond, this diagnosis has brought unexpected gifts…but more on these later.

Since I've been outspoken (moderately and with respect) and have offered interviews, articles, recipes, and help to others along the way, many parents have come to me for advice through the years…perhaps the educator/author combination had something to do with that as well. So as a little side project, I decided to gather everything I knew, dig further into what I didn't know, and write it all down to provide a bit of a shortcut for other parents facing the same circumstance. In other words, I decided to write the book that I wished I'd had at the very beginning. And that, my friends, is how I came to be the Gluten-Free Parent.

The brief version of our story in pictures follows; in the meantime, thank you so much for joining me here! I hope to inspire you towards your own healthy, and yes, happy journey.

To our children's health, and to our own,

Elyn Joy

Edyth's Story

At age 3, Edyth was a normal, happy toddler. Her favorite foods were macaroni and cheese, gluteny-French toast, and popsicles.

By age 8, Edyth's growth had slowed, and she was falling well behind her peers. Over the next year, her growth would slow to a near halt. We were both stumped and worried.

Although she still took part in activities, Edyth lost weight and lacked her usual vibrant energy. She had only mild intestinal symptoms but frequent headaches. At last, her doctor had her tested and discovered her celiac disease.

After the diagnosis and diet change, Edyth's health improved dramatically. In one year, she rebounded in height and had a new glow, seen left after her Nutcracker performance at age 12. A few years later (above right), she would play the leading role as the Sugarplum fairy.

Today (right), Edyth is a luminous and confident college-bound senior who plans to be a neuroscience pre-med major.

INTRODUCTION:
ACCEPTING THE NEW REALITY AS A PARENT
(Because YOUR Acceptance will Lead to your Child's Acceptance)

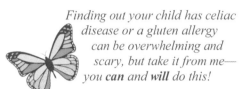

*Finding out your child has celiac disease or a gluten allergy can be overwhelming and scary, but take it from me— you **can** and **will** do this!*

You just learned that your child has celiac disease or a gluten intolerance. On one hand, life as you knew it is over. No more thoughtless food purchases, no dinners at friends' without label-reading, no spontaneous snacking at Disneyland…you get the idea. The biggest difference you will find from start to finish (which, by the way, may be never), is this: You must now and always be MINDFUL of the food you offer your child.

Now, this may sound treacherous to anyone who has taken on a fast-food lifestyle with their children, but there's another less daunting side to the situation, and that is this: Mindfulness is GOOD. Yes, even when it comes to food…for you will now join the ranks of those foodie-types who consider every ingredient before consuming. You'll be able to relate to that parent who follows the vegan/macro diet to the last detail (Gwyneth-style), as well as to the one whose child could suffocate from even the scent of a peanut.

Don't get me wrong—this adjustment is going to require some resiliency, a sense of humor, and perhaps even a few errors at the beginning. When my daughter was diagnosed with celiac at age 9, I thought the world was ending. I mean, how can you explain to a 9 year-old that she can have neither pizza nor birthday cake at her friend's birthday party, or for that matter, at anyone's birthday party, perhaps ever again. You can't.

And there's no denying the heartbreak and guilt that comes with these truths. Our kids want to be kids. We want them to be kids. But when it comes to celiac, we want them to be healthy and to grow—to avoid future disease, or present distress—far more than we care about cake.

So let the transition begin, and be open to it. Know that you are doing your best to pave the way for your child's future life as a gluten-free adult, that your attitude will transfer to your child perhaps as much as will the food she eats.

Children are resilient; they will be fine. It's the adults around them who need to adjust, and quickly!

Finally, before we go on, let me reassure you of something very important: All is not lost. As cliché as that may sound, it has never been truer than now. Most everything your child enjoyed once can still be enjoyed. In fact, you will see that many positives will likely come from this change. The silver lining may even turn out to be gold…but I will explain more about this later.

For now, let's gear up and begin the journey to health, inside and out. It starts right here, right now, and with YOU.

More Thoughts on Acceptance

1) ***Realize that** you cannot change the diagnosis. A medical condition is what it is, at least for now. (Research is fierce in the area of celiac disease, so you never know what the future holds, and yes—let's hold out hope for a cure!)*
2) *ACTION is your best medicine (and your child's as well!). The more you act to pave the way for your child's health, the more in control you will feel.*
3) *Know that your child will react WITH you; therefore, you must remain calm, supportive, and optimistic.*
4) *Fear of the unknown will lessen in direct proportion to your ability to accept, learn, and act.*

I.

Home Safe Home!

STEP 1:
A SAFE HOME IS A
(MUCH) HAPPIER HOME!

A STEP-BY-STEP GUIDE
FOR THE BUSY PARENT

(STRICT version;
MODERATE version follows)

Once you've received a diagnosis of celiac disease or a gluten allergy, the safety of your child's living space is best addressed without delay. You can work more on the acceptance aspect as you move forward.

Transforming your kitchen into a gluten-free-safe zone is much easier than you might imagine. Yes, you will need to weed out many an item if you're like most families. On the positive side, you'll learn a lot in the process—including (and I speak from experience) how many fillers and chemical ingredients you may have been feeding yourself and your family for years.

So off we go….You'd best put on some old, comfie sweats and get ready to clear and clean. I'll take you through the steps required to create a safe and healthy kitchen for your newly-gluten-free child, all while maintaining a productive and well-stocked kitchen for everyone in the home.

SURFACES

✓ *Clean countertops, stovetops, tables, and cutting surfaces using a clean sponge and detergent or an antibacterial, food-safe cleaning solution. Cutting boards that have been used for gluten-containing bread products should be thoroughly sanitized. Consider replacing these with new, unused boards, especially if they are made of a porous material such as wood, or if they are heavily scarred (cracks can hide gluten).*

✓ *Any home with non-gluten-free family members may choose to reserve a zone for "contraband," as my husband likes to call it. This area (which may include a counter and/or cabinets) will be designated for gluten-containing items. Be sure to instruct all family members to keep the space clean with a separate (designated) sponge and towel.*

APPLIANCES

✓ ***MICROWAVE:*** *Thoroughly wash both the outside and inside of your microwave. Use hot water and a sanitizing/antibacterial detergent.*

✓ ***REFRIGERATOR/FREEZER:*** *This is a big job, but you can do a quick clean to get started. Remove items and wipe down shelves and walls. Designate the bottom shelf as the "contraband" shelf, if you choose to keep gluten-containing ingredients. As you begin to learn more about what does and does not contain gluten, you will make decisions about what to keep and what to throw away or donate to a neighbor or friend. To start, read labels and put anything that does not have a "GF" label on a shelf for further research. Those items that are safe may be replaced in the fridge. A general rule: Always store gluten-containing items UNDER those that are safe to better avoid spillage or cross-contamination. Remember that most juices, milks, dairy products, and whole foods (fruits and vegetables) are naturally gluten-free.*

✓ ***OVEN:*** *Wipe out your oven if there are any gluten-containing crumbs on the shelves or the bottom surface. Go over everything with an anti-bacterial detergent or oven cleaner. Run the oven on self-clean if you have that setting; otherwise, turn your oven on the highest setting (often 500 degrees), and keep it on at that temperature for 15-20 minutes. While heat will not entirely remove gluten, it will help turn it to ash to be more effectively wiped away. Once cool, do a last clean wipe of all oven surfaces.*

✓ ***TOASTER OR TOASTER OVEN:*** *These items, if used for gluten-containing bread products, must be parted with. Sorry, but safety is always your priority, and any and all heavily-"glutened" items are not worth the potential risk they present. Of course you may choose to keep them in your designated "contraband" area; otherwise, please invest in a designated gluten-free toaster for your child's safety.*

Sometimes it's better to start over with a safer option. That saying, "Better safe than sorry," becomes critical when it comes to gluten.

✓ ***GRIDDLE AND WAFFLE IRON:*** *You will have to decide whether or not either is worth keeping for gluten-free use. At the very least it will need a thorough scrubbing; however, if your waffle iron has stuck-on batter from past batches of gluten waffles, you are far better off replacing it. Some families keep both gluten-free and non-gluten-free appliances in different cabinets. Be sure to keep all non-safe items stored and marked clearly.*

✓ **DISHWASHER:** *Run your dishwasher on the hottest cycle, ideally using a dishwasher cleaner. The new rule, if washing with gluten-contaminated dishes: Always pre-clean dishes or pots beforehand, and use the "sani" cycle. If your kitchen becomes 100% gluten-free, this is unnecessary. We always recommend saving water where we can.*

✓ **GRILL:** *Scrub grills thoroughly to remove any sign of gluten, then run on the highest heat setting for 10-15 minutes before scrubbing again. At our home, we use one side of the grill for gluten-free items only. Never grill for your gluten-free child on the same surface as gluten-containing products without a thorough re-cleaning.*

A QUICK NOTE ABOUT LABELS....

Certified

GF ®

Gluten-Free

At left is a "Certified Gluten-Free" symbol you will find on many foods that have been tested and certified by one of a handful of accredited organizations. To be safe for consumers with celiac disease, most require a reading of <20 ppm in the USA. Some companies will simply print "Gluten-Free" on their labels; read up on labeling guidelines to become well-informed here or while traveling.

Not all gluten-free foods are labeled, as it costs companies a pretty penny to get tested and labeled. Read the print if you don't see this sign; ingredients that are not gluten-free will be listed by law. Sometimes you'll see "No gluten ingredients" with or without "Produced on equipment that handles wheat," which in some cases is a red flag. Therefore to be 100% safe, we recommend that you buy only certified gluten-free packaged products when possible.

FOOD STORAGE (CABINETS AND PANTRY)

✓ **EMPTY** *cabinets and wipe clean.*

✓ *Check labels of items, and (if you choose to keep them) store anything containing wheat, barley, unlabeled oats, rye, spelt, barley, malt, unlabeled caramel color, or other suspicious products on the LOWEST shelves. As mentioned earlier, should anything spill, this will prevent cross-contamination.*

✓ *For a thorough list of naturally gluten-free foods, as well as many packaged items, check updated lists on the Celiac Disease Foundation's website (see "Resources" in Step 5).*

✓ *Some pantry items will be naturally gluten-free if without additives. This includes canned vegetables and fruits, as well as nuts, seeds, and dried fruits. Also, beans, rice, lentils, millet, corn, and oats are naturally gluten-free, but again—always check labels for potential cross-contamination. About oats: Sometimes the processing leaves them contaminated with gluten; therefore, they MUST be labeled to be safe.*

✓ *Consider switching to gluten-free spices, though this is not a "must do," since most spices are inherently gluten-free. I'm the kind of person who sometimes goes a bit overboard, so we've replaced ours with certified brands. The brand Spicely makes them in cute little green boxes, in case you like the idea.*

MEDICATIONS

✓ **MEDICATIONS:** *Check all medications your child is taking to ensure they are gluten-free. If you are unsure about prescription meds, a call to the pharmacy will tell. These days, most prescribed medications are gluten-free, but I have learned to always ask. Over-the-counter medicines, including acetaminophen, ibuprofen, cough medicines, etc., are available in certified GF versions. In Colorado, the King Soopers stores carry Kroger brand versions of most of these—and they are largely gluten-free. Check Amazon if you don't have Kroger where you live.*

BATH/PERSONAL PRODUCTS

✓ **BATH & PERSONAL PRODUCTS:** *Most doctors agree that gluten will not be absorbed through skin. That said, there's a slim possibility that a child may accidentally swallow a bit of shampoo, conditioner, or bath soap while cleaning up. Therefore, I prefer to purchase gluten-free products for bath and personal care. We use Desert Essence shampoos and conditioners (highly recommended, yummy-smelling, and all labeled GF!) and 365 (Whole Foods) brand foaming cleanser for hands (also labeled GF). That said, doctors agree that these products needn't be certified to be safe but suggest reading labels and choosing products that do not contain gluten ingredients if mouth contact is possible. As for toothpaste, Tom's natural toothpaste is certified gluten-free, and there are others.*

✓ **MAKEUP:** *If you have a teenage girl with a gluten intolerance, you'll be happy to know that several companies are now making GF products. Medical experts assert that products do not have to be gluten-free unless they are worn directly on the mouth. We switched ours to all GF anyway (that overboard gene at play again, I suppose). A few of our favorites are Pacifica and Mineral Fusion, but there are a number of others out there. Eos has lovely and flavorful glosses that Edyth and her friends adore.*

REVIEW: CHECKLIST FOR A SAFE HOME

☐ **SURFACES:** All kitchen surfaces have been cleaned and designated for gluten-free or non-gluten-free. Clean sponges and towels are assigned for gluten-free areas.

☐ **APPLIANCES:** All appliances have been cleaned thoroughly. Those with remaining gluten are either designated for non-gluten-free cooking OR have been removed.

☐ **FOOD STORAGE:** Cabinets are cleaned and marked clearly. Gluten-containing items are either removed or placed on the LOWEST shelves in cabinets and pantries.

☐ **MEDICATIONS:** Current medications have been checked (prescription); over-the-counter meds have been exchanged for labeled or researched gluten-free versions.

☐ **PERSONAL/BATH/HEALTH PRODUCTS:** All have been checked and replaced if needed, including toothpaste, shampoos, soaps, detergents, makeup, etc.

☐ **PET FOOD:** No need to put pets on a gluten-free diet, of course; however, from now on, if your child is feeding pets gluten-containing foods, he should wear gloves or wash hands immediately after handling the food.

MODIFICATIONS

FOR LESS SEVERE ALLERGIES
OR LIFESTYLE/HEALTH CHOICES

o **SURFACES:** Designation may not be necessary; however, be sure to use clean cutting-boards and surfaces for gluten-free food preparation.

o **APPLIANCES:** Ovens and other appliances may be okay to use for moderating gluten. I would still recommend a gluten-free toaster and/or toaster oven, since these tend to harbor the most contamination. Also, avoid making gluten-containing pancakes or waffles on the same equipment without cleaning them first. A good rule of thumb (in a mixed gluten/non-gluten kitchen) is to make the gluten-free items first, then follow up with the rest.

o **FOOD STORAGE:** Be sure to mark gluten-containing items clearly. You may want to still designate a shelf for these items or for those that are gluten-free.

o **MEDICATIONS:** This will be up to you in light of the extent of the gluten avoidance. The GF versions of over-the-counter drugs are easy enough to replace, so why not?

o **PERSONAL/BATH/HEALTH PRODUCTS:** This is the area that will provide you with much more freedom if the avoidance is moderate. You may be fine with all your existing bath and personal products, especially since they are not being eaten purposefully and there's no skin allergy. Be mindful of that possibility, and make your decisions accordingly.

o **PET FOOD:** Gluten from pet food shouldn't bother a child with a mild/moderate allergy; however, we still recommend gloves and good handwashing practices if hands come in contact with food.

❖ ❖ ❖ ❖ ❖ ❖ ❖

Dotted i's and Crossed t's:
No Stone Unturned on the Domestic Front!

We talked about the food, but don't forget about those cat (or dog) treats! Your child should always wash hands after treating her pets. Here, the family cats anticipate their (gluten-based) snacks, along with a little catnip, post-catnap!

As we mention in Step 2 (school considerations), sometimes toys can be culprits as well. Play-Doh and other clay-type substances may contain gluten, so always check with the company or have your child wear gloves while playing with them. Here, brother Oliver as a little one—always building and creating. Today he's an architecture major...no surprise!

When your child has a playdate, be sure to inform the other parent of the gluten-free situation. Even a tea party with Dolly and her friends could prove harmful if gluten-filled mini-cakes or cookies end up on fingers (which can end up in mouths). Always volunteer to provide the tea-cakes and hand wipes if the party is not at your home.

II.

Learn More, TOGETHER

STEP 2:

LEARNING TOGETHER TOWARDS DEEPER UNDERSTANDING AND ACCEPTANCE

Now that your home is safe, the healing process may begin. Yet as we all know, your child's life at home can only help so much…eventually, he or she will venture out— to school, to parties, to afternoons with friends, then to college and beyond (more on this later). Thus, acceptance is not optional—it is absolutely essential. So how do you help a person still growing and learning about self-acceptance in general learn to accept a lifestyle change this sweeping?

In this section, we'll cover the main areas that need to be addressed in order for your child to better understand and accept his or her condition. I will share some of the strategies we used in our own home as well as methods used by friends and others in the community. We will anticipate the questions that may be asked and try to provide you with some perspective on the ways you might best answer them.

Most important is that you remain vigilant and committed towards helping your child reach the next level of understanding, and then the next. Some children will rebel and hide gluten-containing snacks or foods in their rooms. Others will seem to understand but may become overly tempted when pizza arrives at the house or when Auntie Erika's brownies are left out after the party. The result? Either an overtly sick child, or one who remains outwardly all right but who ends up showing symptoms of internal damage at checkup time. (Reactions vary from child to child, as your health provider will attest.)

For this reason, we will focus heavily on the notion of self-advocacy, not only in the community sense, but also in the truest sense of taking charge of one's own health, even—and especially—when no one's looking. For in life, we all must first understand ourselves and our own condition; from there, we may begin to understand the world.

Important Tips to Keep in Mind During the Transition:

 ## LEARN THE FACTS, AND SHARE THE LEARNING.

Learn more about your child's condition and the reason he or she is unable to (or advised against) eating gluten. Get to the SCIENCE of the matter. We've provided a simplistic diagram for you to share with your child on page 18—a place to start, but we recommend further bolstering your child's understanding through the myriad sources available, including those provided by The National Celiac Association, for starters. Share what you learn openly and honestly. Our children have a right to know the truth about their bodies when it comes to allergies or sensitivities. Make it a fun learning opportunity if you can; you can even spark an interest in science and biology while you're learning together!

 ## LET YOUR CHILD ASK ANY QUESTION, THEN HELP HER FIND THE ANSWER.

Whether you access a book, magazine, or a gluten-free forum, do your best to answer your child's initial questions. For those yet unknown, promise to stand by your child while he eventually discovers the answer.

 ## KEEP ROUTINES AS NORMAL AS POSSIBLE.

Although you will need to devote time to the necessary safety measures, try not to fixate on the big change in other areas of your home life. Instead, continue to honor household routines, even as that requires you to change shopping and cooking habits. Make your child's life feel like little, if anything, has changed. He or she will find greater adjustments needed in the outside world, so this stability will help tremendously.

 ## DO NOT DISPLAY PITY FOR YOUR CHILD!

As serious as the health matter may be, it is not the time for outward pity (even though you and your child will of course feel some of that—I know we did). Your job is to educate and support, ***not to produce more anxiety***. Listen, understand, and then encourage acceptance and action.

This in mind, it's natural for a person of any age to mourn something they are losing or have lost. Give your child time to work through these feelings while you continue to provide and encourage other forms of joy and excitement during the transition weeks.

SELF-ADVOCACY IS THE NEW #1 SKILL TO TEACH.

From now on, your child's ability to self-advocate takes center stage when it comes to social skill-building. This will be easier for older kids, but even a kindergartner can learn how to tell someone his or her dietary needs. For younger children, consider making or purchasing some ***"Gluten-Free, Please"*** cards (see p. 25) that they can keep in backpacks. A card or note will alert parents/teachers/field-trip leaders, etc., to the situation.

Older children may benefit from a card as well for use in restaurants or while on vacation; they should also be prepared to speak directly with chefs or food providers about their needs if needed. In any case, make self-advocacy a top priority for any child with a food sensitivity of any kind.

PREPARE YOUR CHILD TO HANDLE PEER PRESSURE SHOULD IT ARISE.

Most of your child's friends and classmates will understand the situation and will be supportive. That said, many children do face peer pressure now and then—often not meant to be malicious but rather stemming from ignorance, as the following story illustrates:

My daughter was once invited to join the gang in eating homemade cupcakes in celebration of a friend's birthday. After Edyth declined to eat one, the friend (a fellow 5th grader) even went so far as to claim they were gluten-free. Edyth relented, thinking her friend knew what she was talking about. What followed was an awful night of stomach and head pains, followed by a dreadful missed day of school and several more days of feeling *blah*. Lesson learned: **Stand up for yourself, and insist on reading a label before eating ANYTHING.** *No label means no way.* And if anyone tries to pressure you to eat something against your will, that person must be removed from your good friend list. True friends never behave this way.

SUPPORT YOUR CHILD THROUGH ALL THE STAGES.

Let's be honest: This is not an easy transition, and ups and downs are bound to happen. Allow your child to cry, to feel sad, and to experience the loss aspect of this new life. Just remind her that the sun is still there, even through the clouds and rain. And when she sees it and begins to get the hang of all the growth aspects of the experience, notice these positive changes and encourage them. The roller-coaster will even out soon enough.

GLUTEN SENSITIVITY and CELIAC DISEASE
A Simplified Primer to Share with Your Child

(Basic facts from The **National Celiac Foundation**. For a more thorough version, please visit celiac.org.)

1) WHAT IS GLUTEN?
Gluten is a protein found in wheat, barley, and rye.

2) WHY IS IT BAD FOR SOME PEOPLE?
People with gluten allergies or sensitivities react to this protein in various ways—from hives to stomach issues to a host of other unwelcome reactions. In people with celiac disease, the protein leads to an immune response wherein a person's small intestine becomes damaged. The damage in the small intestine makes it difficult for the person to absorb vitamins and nutrients. This can lead to vitamin and mineral deficiencies, slowed growth, stomach issues, headaches, or other negative effects.

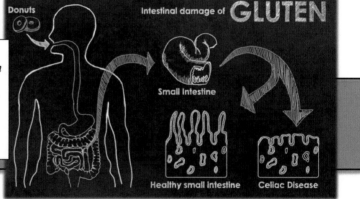

This diagram shows how gluten damages the villi on the intestinal lining. Villi are little projections that "grab" nutrients so that the body can absorb them properly.

3) DO I HAVE TO AVOID GLUTEN COMPLETELY?
If you have a gluten sensitivity or allergy, avoiding gluten is very important. For celiac disease, **a 100% gluten-free diet is your ONLY option to stay safe!** Even a small amount of gluten can cause the kind of damage you see in the above diagram. This isn't an "If I feel like it…" situation—this is your new mindset: NEVER TAKE A CHANCE if you don't know that something is gluten-free. Trust me—the price could be days of feeling icky, and longer periods without proper nutrient absorption!

4) WHAT FOODS MAY CONTAIN GLUTEN THAT ISN'T OBVIOUS?
Many, many foods that are processed and/or that have a long list of ingredients may have gluten hiding in them. From caramel coloring to malt extract to cross-contaminated drinks or grains (such as a uncertified oats), gluten can be pretty sneaky. ALWAYS look for gluten-free certified foods, or choose whole foods (fruits, veggies, rice, beans, unprocessed meats, etc.) that are naturally gluten-free. Next, let's be "Gluten Detectives" and find out more about where it may be hiding.

Let's Be Gluten Detectives: A Game to Play at the Store

As we discussed before, gluten can be pretty sneaky. Let's find out where it may be hiding so that you'll be better prepared to make decisions about what is safe and what is not.

1) **Wheat** comes in many forms. A few of the most familiar forms are listed here (there are more—if in question, look it up before buying/eating!):

   - Couscous
   - Durum
   - Graham
   - Spelt
   - Kamut
   - Seitan

2) **Barley** also has different forms. Often the label will say **MALT**.

3) **Rye** is usually found in bread products and generally does not come in any other form.

Take a field trip to the store with your child. Practice reading labels and deciding whether or not something is gluten-free. Make it a game, with the "gluten detective" being allowed to choose three fun/healthy foods they'd like to take home. Be sure to check the "Contains…" statements as well as the statements about shared equipment (if listed) and facility information. Never be afraid to call a company if you have questions about their product.

Some of the other HIDDEN sources of gluten commonly found:

- Soup broth, bouillon, mixes
- Sauces, gravy
- **Soy sauce** (use GF tamari!)
- Lots of candy (always check labels!)
- Some teas or flavored coffees
- Ready-made marinades
- Meats or cheeses with additives
- Salad dressings
- Prepared seafood items
- Beef jerkys or bacon bits
- Vitamins
- Herbal supplements
- Matzoh, communion crackers
- Seasoned rice dishes
- Nuts (cross contamination/seasonings)
- Medicines (drugstore, prescription)

Cross-Contamination—An Important Reminder for this Game:
*Always check to see if the label says, "Processed **on equipment shared** with wheat" because that is a big RED FLAG. Sometimes items **made in a facility** with wheat will be okay, but you must decide if it's worth the risk. To me, it's not!*

QUESTIONS

Your Child May Ask… and Our Best Answers

Will my celiac disease go away, and will I ever be "normal" again?

A: There are many talented, excited doctors working on ways to help people with celiac. For now, the only cure for this condition is to stop eating gluten. The good news is that there are many kinds of "normal," and most important is the fact that you are still the same YOU, even if you eat a little differently than before!

What about my friends…will they think I'm weird?

A: Remember, in most any group there are kids who have nut allergies, dairy allergies, and all sorts of other issues with food, probably even right in your class or school. And beyond food, some people have asthma, or diabetes, or other conditions that they must deal with every day. Do you think they are weird? Of course not! Now you will understand the challenges of others better, which will help you become a more understanding friend and person! If anyone does not understand and support you, they were not your friend to begin with.

What if I just decide not to follow the diet and keep eating as I have (when no one's looking)?

A: You will hurt yourself from the inside out. Whether or not you feel icky (which you probably will—and possibly for days), you will hurt your body. You may lose some of your height as an adult, and you may get sick with other diseases because your body will become weaker. This is a "no cheating allowed" kind of change—and you will have to become your own "police" to enforce the rules!

...but what about

PARTIES??

...or *holidays* ***or*** *events* ***or*** *banquets* ***or*** *field trips* ***or*** *prom* ***or...?***

ALL-TIME Best Answer:

"We go to events for the PEOPLE and EXPERIENCES, rather than for the FOOD."

"Never go to a party or event hungry. That way, if there's nothing gluten-free, you can play, sip juice or another safe drink, and enjoy the company."

Another FAVORITE:

"Take mental notes of the fun things to eat at the party, then come home so we can plan to make some of them this week!"
(We did this right after a party wherein our daughter was longing for a cake pop. Ours were more like frosted cake-squares with sticks, but they were yummy, and she was thrilled!)

"If you know you will want a bite at the party, be a **snack-sneaker**. *Smuggle in your own snack, then play a game to see if anyone even notices that you're eating your own food instead of the party food—usually they won't."*

A Note on the "Teen Scene" with Celiac Disease

On pages 37-38 of this book, our teen daughter reflected on the many ways she grew and became a "better person" (her words) through and because of her celiac disease. Much of this had to do with self-advocating and taking control of her own safety--she was encouraged to grow in ways her friends were not. Sure, once in awhile she felt a little left out when everyone else was ordering pizza, but she persevered, had lots of (GF) parties at our home, and learned to value friends and experiences above all!

III.

You, Me, and the Great Wide World

STEP 3:
NAVIGATING IN A GLUTEN-FILLED WORLD

Always come prepared...and should you discover that you didn't need to,

what a lovely surprise it will be!

Let's see how far we've come to get to this step: First, we received the news and allowed ourselves a bit of space to let it sink in. We didn't wait long, though, before we rounded the corner into action. We cleaned our kitchen, replaced food and other items, and created a safe home for our child and family. From there, we fielded questions, shared in research and exploration with our child, and touched on some of most important aspects of learning how to accept this new course. And, when the moments of sadness and mourning arose, we allowed them to be experienced while committing to the sunnier side of life as they passed.

Now, we must face the world in a real way. Neither we—nor our children—should live in fear of the great wide world. If anything, being gluten-free should become yet another adventure, another horizon to explore, a challenge in the quest akin to Columbus's unpredictable sea or Frank Lloyd Wright's spatial enigma. Thus one simple answer will not fit all situations. That said, I can offer you some helpful tips for facing ordinary situations, as well as a few more for the less common waves you may encounter while sailing your own ship out there.

*Learn to know when to say **Yes**, when to say **No**, and when to do a little more research.*

"To-Do" Lists for Those Worldly Pursuits

Checklist for School and Community Groups

☐ **Alert teachers, group leaders, and counselors** to the new dietary protocol. You will need to update medical forms and information for your child.

☐ **Schedule a meeting with those who work most closely with your child.** Arrange back-up foods or snacks where appropriate. For instance, if your child is in a classroom wherein snacks are scheduled, work with the teacher to create a solution that accommodates your child with the least amount of attention (i.e., gluten-free snacks for all some days, a special stash of snacks similar to those other students will have, etc. Be willing to provide and restock as needed.)

☐ Be sure to **address materials in class that may use gluten-containing items** (such as Play-Doh or cooking activities). Plan to keep in touch with the teacher so that alternative solutions may be mapped out in advance.

☐ If your child eats the school lunch, **meet with the food providers** to check on safety for children with food allergies. Most lunch services will offer a salad or other gluten-free-friendly option; however, the risk for cross-contamination may be high. My recommendation is to do your homework but always go the safest route. For us, that meant a daily packed lunch. (See Step 5 for fun school lunch suggestions.) Always pack plenty of snacks and meals for field or groups trips, too.

☐ **Let your child help plan her own snack and lunch** menus. Taking part in food planning builds confidence and adds a little fun to the challenge!

☐ If your child takes part in sports or after-school activities, be sure have him **keep fruit, protein bars, and/or other snack items** in his backpack (a good idea regardless; a gluten intolerance will NOT slow down that growing-kid eating machine!).

☐ **DON'T panic** or feel you need to monitor your child during the school day (a.k.a. parental stalking; believe me, I know the temptation!). This will only add anxiety to your child and others and will slow down the adjustment process. You will need to trust that he or she will be supported by the adults in charge, learning curve and all.

Birthday Parties, Sleepovers, Friends' Dinners, etc.

- Remember the mantra, and say it again and again: *We go to events for the people and the experiences, not for the food!* Even so, a little food planning is fine and may help your child's feeling of connection at snack/mealtime.

- If possible, **chat with the hosting parent/guardian before the event.** Let them know the situation, and ask about their food-related plans. That way you can plan your bring-along food to coordinate with the existing menu. (For instance, if they are serving chocolate birthday cupcakes, you can make chocolate cupcakes beforehand and send the similar cupcake along with your child.)

- In our experience, other families will sometimes offer to make or serve gluten-free food items. In these cases, it's perfectly acceptable to **mention cross-contamination** to the parent. If they are using clean bowls and metal (not wooden or absorbent) utensils and pans, the food should be okay to eat. Cross-contamination in an oven is rare when foods are baked separately (i.e., no gluten baking while the GF item is baking).

- From a safety standpoint, **always bring your own something**—be it a snack, a course to share with others, a dessert—whatever you think will be most helpful in keeping your child happy at the event.

- Another rule to live by: **Don't go to events hungry!** Always have your child eat a little something (or a full meal, depending on the situation) beforehand. She can also bring a little bite to eat or share with the others, if no GF foods are available. Otherwise, ordering a safe drink and enjoying the company is always a-okay!

- As mentioned earlier, consider making or purchasing **"Gluten-Free, Please!" calling cards** for your child to give to anyone serving him food (available at glutenfreeparent.com).

- Remember: **No social situation is worth days of illness!**

*The Gluten-Free Parent's **"Gluten-Free, Please"** calling cards are great for kids to keep in their backpacks or purses. Your child can share them anytime they are in an unfamiliar situation wherein food will be served. These are helpful to have at restaurants, too!*

When it's Your Child's Happy Birthday

When it's your turn to throw the party, worry not—you can create a 100% safe, gluten-free celebration worthy of the history books without much trouble at all! Here are some quick tips on how to go about planning and executing the festivities. I'll also leave you with a list of themed parties we held for our kids; and, even though Edyth's brother Oliver didn't have to be gluten-free, we kept his parties safe for his sister, too.

❖ Everyone knows that **the birthday cake is the main event**, right? So make it a new tradition to create one for your child using the theme of his/her choice! Of course, it may not turn out as polished as will a bakery version (and if you have access to a GF bakery, that's always an option), but there's something about a homemade cake that's just special. We have made all sorts of GF cakes for both kids, minus the fancy frosting décor, and the kids have always loved them.

  o To start, **let your child choose the flavor/type of cake**. My kids have asked for carrot cake, cheesecake, ice cream cake, strawberry cake, chocolate cupcakes, and even a confetti cake (that was the Barbie cake).

  o **Decorate the cake** with fruits, edible flowers, or little toys (washed thoroughly, of course), or make a shape out of the cake. If you're a fancy-frosting sort of baker, I'm jealous. The most we drew on anyone's cake was their name and a not-so attractive attempt at a daisy.

  o Here are **a few of our cake themes through the years**: Rocket Cake (stacked cakes with a cone on top), Barbie Cake (the skirt was a bundt cake, the torso rose through frosting), Hot Wheels Cake (we made a chocolate road on the white icing—impressive, huh?), Fairy Cake (lots of sparkly sugar and miniature fairies, trees, and green frosting), Lego Cake (with real Legos for décor, of course), and fancy square tea cakes with sugar flowers (we made the petit fours and bought sugar flowers).

❖ As for the rest of the party, you can take the cake to the bowling alley, mini-golf course, or park and **proceed as with any party**, or you can host a theme party at your house. Edyth's all-time favorite was the dressed-up tea party she had for her 12th birthday. The girls all came in dresses, and we made finger sandwiches on gluten-free bread with cute toothpicks holding them together… and then there were those tea cakes, and of course, mint tea!

❖ A few **foods that translate well to a birthday party** (see the meals in Step 5 for more): taco/burrito bar, pasta bar, GF pizza, sandwiches, popcorn, GF candy, tortilla chips & salsa, GF pretzels, popcorn, popsicles, veggies & dips.

Overnight Field Trips or Summer Camps

☐ **Assess whether or not the trip will be safe for your child.** This is a difficult and sometimes painful need—because in truth, not every longer camp experience will be worth the risk. See Step 5's "Resources" section for *Gluten-Free Living*'s list of GF camps in the US.

☐ **Connect with leaders and kitchen staff** (if applicable) before any overnight or longer trip. Have them walk you through a typical menu, and ask if they may be able to incorporate a few of your child's favorites.

☐ For longer camps, assessing the situation also must include an **evaluation of potential cross-contamination.** For example, if the oven, toaster, and microwave at the camp are used for all foods, this may not be the best place for your child (as they will not be able to eat most hot foods for the duration). Sometimes, the camp will work with you to ensure the child's safety, taking extra measures (such as wrapping GF foods in foil, which should be safe, or boiling gluten-free noodles in separate water, etc.). Take a tour of the kitchen if you think that would help you better gauge the environment.

☐ **If a trip is for just one night, you can avoid pitfalls by packing food** for every meal. Ask for a refrigerator if possible to expand your options packing-wise. The items listed in Step 5's lunch ideas section translate well to short trips. With a fridge/freezer onsite, we've also packed frozen GF ready-made meals (Amy's Kitchen has many of these), mac and cheese, and cold egg or other salads. Again, be sure to remind staff to warm up these meals wrapped in plastic or foil if using a shared microwave or oven! If refrigeration isn't an option, plan to pack a cooler and make sure your child plans to eat chilled items first.

☐ **Include extra snacks**, always. Now and then, consider including a snack for everyone, which will help your child feel part of things—check with the teacher or leader first, of course.

☐ For longer camps or trips, **appoint ONE go-to person** who will be in charge of overseeing the safety of your child. This person should have your direct phone number and should be accompanying your child on excursions (or carefully training another counselor to do so, with your permission) during the camp session.

☐ **Offer to supply gluten-free food items** if that will help keep your child safe. Some camps will have many options already on hand for kids with food allergies or sensitivities; others will recommend that you supply meals, a toaster, or other items.

Traveling with Family: Fun and Safety for All

- **Research safe options** in your destination area. If you are traveling to a city and have a choice between staying across the street from a gluten-free bakery or staying where there are no GF restaurants, well, you know which one to choose. We've planned many hotel stays around the best GF food locations!

- **If you can find a room or space with a kitchen space, jump on it!** Even a kitchenette with a small fridge and cooking space (or microwave) helps. Just make a quick stop at the local market to stock up on a few easy gluten-free meals and snacks. That way, no matter what the day may bring food-wise, your child will always have safe options waiting for him back at the hotel.

- **If you are going somewhere for an outdoor adventure (such as camping), load up on your gluten-free must-haves before you leave town.** Purchase perishable foods as close to the destination as possible, and bring plenty of ice.

- **Keep a few extra snacks in your daypack** while touring. These days, many popular destinations offer gluten-free options (calling ahead will help you locate the best spots). That said, sometimes a great trip calls for spontaneity and exploration…so you never know. Plan accordingly.

- If you are staying in an all-inclusive resort, **ask for a guided tour** of the buffet lines on the first day. Most resorts will have an English-speaking chef or manager who can show you where to find the best gluten-free options. Our family has stayed in a few resorts where the chef even made and hand-delivered special foods to our daughter at each meal! You won't know what's available until you ask. So don't be shy—people really do want to help!

- **Choose the safest option for the gluten-free child often**, and make it an adventure for everyone. The ***findmeglutenfree*** app is an excellent resource for domestic travel—it will help you find the nearest GF eating spots in a flash. Finally, should family members long for that famous local (unsafe) pizza spot, let them enjoy that—your GF child will learn to compromise and just sit back and enjoy the company at these times, with her own special treat to come.

Notes & Tips for Safe Eating in Restaurants

➢ **Consider the type of food being served** when choosing your restaurants. For instance, the following food categories are generally gluten-free (with exceptions, so always check): Indian dishes, Thai curries, Mexican foods with corn tortillas, fresh Greek, Israeli, and Mediterranean fare, sushi (with tamari or GF soy sauce), salad bars (minus croutons), many vegan dishes, and more. Even if you think you know something is safe, always ask servers to please alert the chef of your situation and encourage a double-check of ingredients and practices.

➢ If you walk into a restaurant and **the servers have not heard of gluten-free, choose another restaurant**. This happened to us in New York in a couple of different small restaurants—holes in the wall, so to speak. We found suitable alternatives within a couple of blocks.

➢ **Never be afraid to ask about cross-contamination and about the safety measures** (if any) practiced by kitchen staff to protect gluten-free patrons. For example, many pizza spots now offer gluten-free pizza crusts; however, some of them prepare their GF pizzas in the same location as they do the wheat-based pizzas. Imagine the flour flying back there; this may well result in a sick child! We have gone out for pizza on a few occasions, but only where the kitchen staff takes great care to separate both the preparation and the cooking of the pizzas. Even the tabletop upon which you eat should be double-checked for crumbs or other gluten-containing remnants.

➢ **If the menu says "gluten-free," it's still wise to investigate further.** As shared above, that means asking about prep surfaces, kitchen staff hygiene (do they change gloves?), fresh pans and water for pasta (or oil for frying), clean utensils, and even sources/labeling of GF food. Most restaurants are happy to answer these questions.

➢ At walk-through Mexican-style buffet spots wherein both gluten-loaded and gluten-free options are available, **always ask for servers to change their gloves**. Sometimes such places will also use new utensils for gluten-free orders.

➢ As mentioned earlier, **the *findmeglutenfree* app** can guide you to local GF restaurants; however, it doesn't always include every option. That in mind, it's a good place to start, especially if you are traveling. New gluten-free spots and menus are popping up every day, so check online, or ask around to stay current.

➢ The bottom line: **Find your safe spots, and stick to them.** And if you happen to be somewhere questionable with a hungry family, order a safe side or drink for your GF child, and break out those always-ready snacks until you can find a better alternative later. Most importantly, be sure to let **your child practice doing all of the above on her own.** That's how you teach self-advocacy, our #1 goal through all this!

Thoughts on Launching Your GF Child (to college and beyond)

- More and more colleges are taking the gluten-free (and allergy-conscious) diet seriously. **Do your research to find out which ones stand out in helping students stay safe**. Some campuses may have gone through gluten-free certification programs or may even feature dedicated dining halls.

- Make **touring the dining facilities** a must on any college visit. Note the arrangement of options and the existence (or nonexistence) of proper labeling.

- If possible, **meet or speak with a representative in food services** for your selected school. Make a list of questions around food preparation, serving, and cross-contamination. See if the school is able to fulfill special requests—important if, like my daughter, your child has additional restrictions. In our case, Edyth is happiest to know she can always stick to her gluten-free-vegan diet by ordering a baked potato or having an excellent and safe salad bar available any time.

- I strongly recommend **requesting a small fridge and microwave** for your child's dorm room. This way, he can store snacks or easy "to-go" meals for times when an event fell short on the gluten-free front, or for late nights when restaurants and dining halls are closed. Make sure your child has a way to get to a grocery or natural foods store regularly to keep that fridge stocked.

- When choosing an ideal school or apartment, **scope out the neighborhood for gluten-friendly restaurants** and coffee shops. Better yet, try to find a home base not too far from a grocery shop that sells ample GF options along with fresh, whole, naturally-gluten-free foods.

- Remember: The greatest gift you can give to any child about to leave the nest is **the gift of SELF-ADVOCACY** we've been discussing through this book. Once instilled and practiced, this ability will allow your child to be able to take care of herself from here on out…the ultimate victory for a gluten-free parent!

A Few More (Somewhat Random) Tips for Enjoying the Great Wide World

- Encourage your child **NOT TO SHARE UNWRAPPED FOOD items**—chips, unwrapped candy, popcorn—with others who are also eating gluten-containing foods. This is less of a party and more of a cross-contamination festival. Let her pour her own servings of each item before others dig in (she'll have to advocate for this…so start at home).

- **TRUST your instincts.** If you aren't sure about a person's knowledge or a place's safety practices, just say no to the food and either arrange for your own or pass on the situation entirely if it's going to compromise your child. This should be true for travels, summer camps, and anything else that's optional. There are enough safe options out there—you just have to commit to finding them!

- **Consider ALL-INCLUSIVE resorts or hotels with buffet restaurants** if that's an option. The more food choices you have, (especially in international travel), and the more you can actually SEE the food or speak with a chef, the less likely you'll be to get sick.

- Some parents have asked if smelling bread will make their child sick. The short answer no, at least not from afar! So go ahead and **ENJOY the sight, sounds, and smells** as you travel. That said, don't encourage your gluten-free child to put his face into the loaf of bread to get a better whiff. Not a good idea.

- **Never stop learning about LABEL-READING**, since laws around GF labeling are constantly changing and evolving. Keep informed by reviewing current labeling standards and become familiar with those used by a foreign country before you travel there.

- When going to restaurants that serve gluten-free dips, salsas, etc., don't hesitate to **BRING YOUR OWN CHIPS or CRACKERS**. This way, you'll be able to enjoy the gluten-free offerings safely, even if the restaurant's own chips/crackers don't measure up. (For instance, some Mexican restaurants will have corn chips; however, they've been fried in oil with other gluten-containing items. This is a big NO, with no exceptions! Politely ask the waitress if you can use your own; I've never heard a "no" to that.)

- For **POTLUCK** events, **ALWAYS BRING A MEAL-EQUIVALENT DISH** to share with its own servingware, and try to get your child through the line early for that and any other safe dish before the risk of cross-contamination rises.

IV.

Behind Every Cloud is a
Brilliant Blue Sky

STEP 4:
ANTICIPATING THE CHALLENGES—AND CELEBRATING THE UPSIDES—OF THE GLUTEN-FREE PARENTING EXPERIENCE

"...And sometimes we have to lose something before we can find ourselves."

-- Bella's Star

From the moment any of us gets the news (about our child's celiac disease or gluten sensitivity), we know that this will not be easy—at least, not initially. In fact, some of us may have suddenly found ourselves identifying with Chicken Little (remember that cartoon character who believed the sky was falling?), imagining the impossibility of it all. Yet last I checked, the sky is still in place, and so are we. Our children are still laughing and growing, and—if we've been vigilant about Steps 1-3—they are likely well on their way to flourishing.

Even so, this book would not be complete without mentioning some of the challenges you will inevitably face. I'd like to say that your child will NEVER be "glutened," as we call it, but that would be a lie. Hopefully, this will happen rarely, very rarely—and maybe you will somehow avoid it and set a world record for the shortest learning curve in gluten-free history. Yet if you're like most of us, it will happen…and when it does, it's important to be prepared.

There are other potential issues, too, that may get in the way of the rainbows-and-sunshine childhood we'd all like our kids to experience. Beyond these pitfalls, however, there are many positives (believe it!) that will bloom from this. We need to remember these and maximize—even celebrate—them.

Ultimately, life would not be life without a measure of loss, challenge, and change. These are the things that lend color and character to our days, difficult as they may sometimes be. And when we learn how to discover more about ourselves through each passage, we gain wisdom. Like the tree, we bend. And we—along with our children—experience the very best thing we can do in this life, which is to *grow*.

When Gluten Happens...

As much as we'd like to believe that we can protect our child 100% of the time, the fact is this: He or she may come in contact with gluten at some point. For us, it happened at least four times during those first couple of years: once at school (the cupcake incident) and a few times at friends' homes when something was prepared in a contaminated space. One time later on, we trusted that pizza menu a little too much, and we didn't bother to learn that the crusts served were made in a facility that also produced wheat. And then there was the "gluten-free" (and label-free) cookie dough I purchased in support of a sports team...well, a nasty migraine and two days of vomiting later, I think we can safely assume that was some serious false advertising.

So what do you do when your child has eaten gluten? It's easy to panic—and I wish I could tell you there's no reason to—but in truth this is serious business and must be avoided if we're to keep our children healthy! Still, panicking is counter-productive, and you don't want to pass on that anxiety to your child; he's already going through the physical repercussions which are punishment enough. Instead, try the following steps that have helped us through. Contact your doctor if the symptoms are extreme or if they last more than a day or so.

1) Keep your child hydrated, especially if she is vomiting or has diarrhea. Bland foods are recommended until the most severe symptoms pass.
2) If your child has a headache, offer a **gluten-free pain medicine** (we use Kroger brand acetaminophen, which is certified GF).
3) **Ginger tea with honey** is known to help calm the stomach. Some parents have suggested chamomile or peppermint tea as well—but please, double check that your tea is also labeled gluten-free. Some companies use gluten-containing glue on tea bags or contain unsafe ingredients. Many (if not all) of Celestial Seasonings teas are certified GF; there are other brands as well.
4) We have used *GlutenEase™* or other **enzymatic supplements** which claim to aid in gluten digestion. That said, current research has not proven such supplements as effective, and some professionals discourage their use entirely. Researchers are working hard on formulating medicines to help prevent gluten reactions—a bright possibility for future relief!
5) Make sure you are keeping your child on a **healthy, nutrient-rich diet supplemented with gluten-free multivitamins** as he heals (and as a general rule!). Be very careful after the gluten exposure; you do not want to increase the damage by having another "slip."

A Few of the Less-Visible Challenges of the Gluten-Free Parenting Experience

Although "getting glutened" is the biggie when it comes to the gluten-free life, there are other less physical and more emotional aspects to being a gluten-free kid that aren't always fun. To be a savvy and supportive gluten-free parent, we need to anticipate these challenges and know how to deal with them when they arise.

➤ At times **your child may feel SAD and SORRY for him/herself**. This is normal. Allow your child to work through these feelings and to talk openly about them. If you think your child's mourning process is affecting the rest of his life adversely, perhaps he would benefit from speaking to a doctor, counselor, or therapist. Some children may have more difficulty adjusting to their new reality than will others. Most will likely have moments of these feelings, which will be balanced with "back to normal" behaviors. Just respect the process and pay attention while providing an understanding ear and lots of reasons to be grateful (try *The Gratitude Game,* below).

➤ You will more than likely encounter times wherein **your child may express that she FEELS LEFT OUT of one activity or another** due to the food situation. Here are some ways to help:

   o Remind your child to remember that **events are always about the people and activities first!**

   o Encourage him to stand strong and to not give in to any peer pressure around food. Help him learn to stay light about the situation around friends. **Keeping a sense of humor will discourage teasing**, because no one likes to make fun of someone who remains unfazed by their attempts.

   o **Host gatherings for your child and her friends**. Make the food preparation exciting by allowing her to choose and/or to cook and bake for the event.

   o For small(er) events, **pack enough fun/yummy gluten-free snacks for your child to share with everyone** who will be there.

   o Play *The Gratitude Game*!

The Gratitude Game

In his book **Celebrate: Lessons Learned from the World's Most Admired Organizations,** *author and speaker Scott Friedman emphasizes the role gratitude plays in helping us create our best lives. He references a game called "The Best of the Best," our inspiration for* **The Gratitude Game,** *in which everyone wins.*

Here's how to play: Every day, ask your child to name three things she is grateful for that day. This "game" works best when everyone in the family is gathered together, so that all can participate and celebrate one another's gratitude lists. By naming what we're grateful for, we are reminded of what we DO have, thus increasing our sense of abundance rather than lack.

...And Yet Still Something *GROWS*...

Call it a silver lining, a bright side, "the other hand," or whatever you wish....The important thing is that we recognize those special gifts that may be hiding just inside of our greatest challenges.

When your child was first diagnosed or otherwise relegated to a strict gluten-free diet, you may have found it easy to jump straight to the negatives—the health matters (no downplaying this one; it's well warranted), what he or she won't be able to eat, which restaurants you'll have to give up, how you'll have to navigate the dangers at school or camp or friends' homes, and so forth. Yet your training wouldn't be complete without a generous mention of the upsides of this whole gluten-free experience!

I know, I know—you're probably thinking, "Upsides? Isn't that just rationalization?" to which I will answer with a passionate NO. I'm being 100% sincere when I say that there ARE some pretty significant positives that have come of this for our daughter. Moreover, we all have learned a lot about nutrition, advocacy, and empathy towards others who have dietary or other restrictions. We've had to hone our skills as parents from virtually every aspect: physical, psychological, social, even spiritual. It's brought our family closer in some ways, especially by encouraging more baking/cooking time together, adventurous restaurant exploration, and mutual empathy and support.

As many leaders and thinkers have said, it's not the challenges which life brings us that define our character; rather, it's what we DO with and about them. And I know this much: the challenges we and Edyth have faced these past several years have tested each one of us in various ways. Yet through it all, it is Edyth who has grown the most, and I have to say—she's not just a survivor, she's an absolute superstar!

In the next pages, I'll share a few of the many upsides that have come from our gluten-free lifestyle changes. No doubt you will experience some of your own, unexpected yet wonderfully welcomed.

Just a Few of the Ways Your Child Can (and likely WILL) Evolve
(Each of these changes in our Edyth was in great part a result of her celiac diagnosis)

❖ DISCIPLINE: What started as a challenge from the outside (i.e., parents and doctors saying, "You must not eat this…" or "You only can have this or that") eventually became a challenge from within. It takes discipline to resist temptation, to remember ingredients and read labels, and to put people and experiences first. For Edyth, this increasing sense of self-control began to surface in other areas of her life. She seemed to become incrementally more disciplined with school, with dance, and even with mundane tasks at home, such as cleaning her room.

We remain convinced that the celiac disease diagnosis fed this aspect of her development in very positive ways, including Edyth's recent foray into the college application and interviewing processes, which she has handled almost 100% on her own!

❖ MINDFULNESS AROUND NUTRITION AND HEALTH MATTERS: Once Edyth got the hang of label-reading and gluten-free safety considerations in food choices, she seemed to become more attuned to healthy eating in general. Like every kid, she loved to enjoy sweets or "junky" GF pretzels or chips now and then, but the leaning towards junk foods slowly shifted towards healthy, sure-thing options fairly early on—maybe within a couple of years.

By her later teens, Edyth's go-to snacks became whole-food items such as peanut butter and bananas, or hummus with snap peas and carrots. She recently remarked about how lucky she felt to have been given the "gift of knowledge about nutrition" all because of her celiac disease. What do you know?!

❖ RESILIENCY: One of the most remarkable and admirable areas of growth exhibited by Edyth around all of this was her sense of resiliency. Even during those tough moments—after a party, or when she felt too sick to stand after an early-on diet slip, this girl bounced back. And that ability to get through tough moments, hours, and days again translated into other aspects of her life. She learned how to dance through life, even after an occasional fall.

In Her Words...

**(Quotes from an interview with Edyth Dae,
college-bound teen who has grown up with celiac disease)**

"All of the negatives I experienced at the beginning got so much easier and better with time. Just be patient, and know that you will find your new normal."

"One of the ways I think I've grown the most is in the area of self-advocacy. Before all this, I didn't know how to express my needs clearly and confidently. It wasn't just about age, either—the gluten-free life pretty much forced me to become my own best advocate for food and other things, too. I think I'm more mature and confident now because of it."

"Being gluten-free has helped me take more responsibility for my own health. Plus I've had fun learning how to cook and bake gluten-free, and I'm excited to get better at it both for myself and for others in the future!"

This whole experience has made me more grateful for the little things in life that I might otherwise have taken for granted. I've learned that the little annoyances just aren't important, because what matters most are health, family, friendships, and finding your passions."

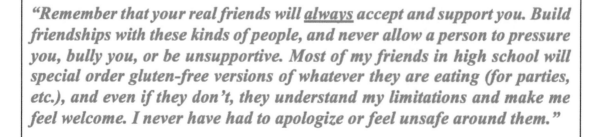

"Remember that your real friends will <u>always</u> accept and support you. Build friendships with these kinds of people, and never allow a person to pressure you, bully you, or be unsupportive. Most of my friends in high school will special order gluten-free versions of whatever they are eating (for parties, etc.), and even if they don't, they understand my limitations and make me feel welcome. I never have had to apologize or feel unsafe around them."

Edyth, growing and bending like a strong tree
(here at age 14, after almost 5 years on a gluten-free diet)

V.

Never Stop Evolving...

STEP 5: EXPAND YOUR REPERTOIRE

TIPS ON COOKING, BAKING, AND MEAL-PLANNING
(PLUS OUR FAVORITE RESOURCES AND RECIPE!)

Congratulations! If you've read this far, you've now become well-acquainted with the first four steps—or aspects—of becoming a confident gluten-free parent, well-equipped to handle the challenges while recognizing and appreciating those unique opportunities for your child's beautiful evolution. Now, the best thing you can do is learn, and then keep learning and growing!

To help in that realm, we've gathered some basic **tips for gluten-free cooking and baking**, including **our list of "must-have" ingredients** for your gluten-free pantry and a primer on some of the most commonly-used gluten-free flours. We'll also cover a few of the **differences and challenges you may encounter** in translating ordinary recipes to gluten-free.

Even though this book is not a recipe book per se, I wanted to provide you with a helping of easy **go-to dinner possibilities** (our family favorites), along with a selection of **Edyth's favorite school lunch picks**.

Finally, we'll direct you to some of the **best gluten-free resources we've found**—from expert organizations, magazines, and cookbooks to blogs, apps, and lifestyle websites. Edyth and I also wanted to share with you our all-time favorite (top secret, or at least it was until now) **vegan-optional gluten-free chocolate-chip cookies recipe**!

Again, we are so grateful that you decided to join us on this journey. As overwhelming as it all may have seemed at first, I hope that by now you've gained a bit of extra knowledge and wisdom to armour yourself in addressing the needs in your own child's world. So here we go, 'round the last stretch for now, and off towards the best possible gluten-free future for our children!

KITCHEN BASICS

Before starting your gluten-free cooking adventure at home, be sure to **review the checklists in Step 1** to ensure a SAFE and CLEAN environment for your safest cooking and baking. This means **NO SHARED SPACES OR EQUIPMENT** unless they have been cleaned and sanitized! Also, by now your toaster, wooden spoons, and other permanently cross-contaminated items should have been replaced.

Along with these safety measures, here's a reminder to replace all your go-to favorite and basic ingredients with gluten-free versions. The following list of pantry essentials will ensure a well-stocked gluten-free kitchen (note the * next to any item means that it should be replaced with only certified or cross-checked gluten-free versions):

- Flour mix* (see our favorite blended flour recipe on the next page)
- Butter, margarine,* cooking oil
- Cocoa* and chocolate chips*
- Coconut*
- Milk or milk substitute*, eggs, cream cheese,* yogurt, other dairy or dairy substitutes*
- Cooking spray
- Herbs and spices*
- Yeast,* baking powder and soda,* cream of tartar*
- Sugars (brown, powdered, granulated)
- Vanilla extract*
- Vinegar (wine, apple cider)*
- Xanthan gum, guar gum
- Cornstarch* and tapioca starch*
- Condiments* -- ketchup, mustard, mayonnaise or Vegenaise™
- Nuts* and nut butters*

- Salsas*
- Olives (black, green, Kalamata)*
- Marinara sauce*
- Rice (brown, white)*
- Oats/oatmeal*
- Pasta*
- Quinoa, millet
- Tortillas,* taco shells*
- Canned tomatoes and beans
- Chicken or vegetarian broth and/or bouillon*
- Bread products*: Bread, pizza crusts, bread mixes, rolls, etc.
- Cereals,* breakfast foods*
- Pancake/waffle mix*
- Meats: Tuna, cut meats, etc.
- Cheeses*
- Salad dressings*
- Fresh fruits, vegetables, and fruit juices

For any of the above items, be sure to double check for gluten a) if there are added spices or seasonings, and b) if you are uncertain for any reason. Check company websites, or ask for clarification via phone.

All Flours are Not Created Equal

To become a well-informed gluten-free cook or baker, we all have to get to know our flour options. Whether creating a blend for cakes or choosing an effective combo for crisp coating and pan-frying, not all GF options will produce the same results. For this reason, let's go through some of the flours available and see how they are best used in recipes. Be sure to read my quick note on gums (see next page recipe) as well.

- **Rice Flour:** Provides a great substitute for white flour; however, I do recommend you use it at a ratio of around 3:1 with a starch, along with a pinch of xanthan or guar gum for best results when baking. **Brown rice flour** is a little thicker and heavier than the white. It can also taste a bit grittier but provides a nice whole-wheat texture when used in recipes in the ratios described above.

- **Buckwheat Flour:** Much denser with a distinct, nutty flavor. Best when used with lighter flours and starches.

- **Coconut Flour:** This is a highly-absorbent flour with a slightly oily texture when used in baking. It gives everything a coconut-y flavor. Best when blended with a starch at approximately 4:1.

- **Almond Meal:** One of our all-time family favorites! It adds moisture, flavor, and texture to baked goods when used with other flours (see Edyth's Best Flour Blend).

- **Potato Flour:** Very light and moist. Can result in a more "gooey" dough, so best used with other flours to balance the starchy effect.

- **Teff, Garbanzo,** and **Quinoa Flours**: Each of these is best used with other flours and starches. By themselves, each has a strong and unique flavor. Try them, as well as other specialty flours, and make your own decisions as to what your family likes best.

- STARCHES: These work as thickening agents in gravies, soups, and casseroles. They are also excellent when blended with other flours, as they help create that binding action missing due to the lack of gluten. Here are a few of the most commonly used starches:

  - ➢ Cornstarch: Great for flour blends and thickening; helps create crispy crusts when used in bread recipes.
  - ➢ Potato Starch: Very light and excellent at retaining moisture in recipes. Recommended for thickening or baking softer items vs. crispy ones.
  - ➢ Tapioca Starch: Excellent as a thickener and an all-purpose starch in flour mixes.

Our Best Gluten-Free Flour Blend
(Use in place of regular flour—our homemade "go to" for baking.)

Ingredients:

- ➢ 2 cups brown or white rice flour
- ➢ 1 cup tapioca starch
- ➢ 1 cup almond meal (okay to replace with another 1 cup rice flour if you are nut-free)
- ➢ ½ cup cornstarch
- ➢ 1 ½ teaspoons xanthan gum*

Place all ingredients in a large bowl and blend thoroughly with a metal whisk or long fork. Store in an airtight container or bag in a cool, dry place.

Quick **Note on GUMS (xanthan, guar): Use these sparingly. They are binders but will end up sticky and gooey if overused! I usually cut the amount mentioned in a recipe down to ½- ¾ per my experience. A little goes a long way!*

And P.S.: We also LOVE Pamela's Gluten-Free Baking & Pancake Mix, even enough to mention it here! If you use it, decrease or remove the leavening ingredients (baking powder or baking soda) in your recipe.

Some General Tips for the Gluten-Free Chef

❖ In general, **gluten-free baking with flour or mixes will be less moist** than will their gluten-filled counterparts. For this reason, we included almond meal/flour in our favorite mix; the almond element adds moisture to the end product. If you choose to forego the nut flour, we recommend adding an extra ½ tablespoon of fat (oil, butter, etc.) to your recipe.

❖ Your gluten-free baked items **may take just a little longer** to bake. Follow directions for recipes and use your cake-tester as needed.

❖ **Many recipes can be modified for gluten-free** once you learn the basic principles. Don't be afraid of a little trial and error! We've called a few of our "experiments" total disasters, but we applied general baking principles to determine what was needed in the repeat attempt.

❖ However, **some things do not translate well to gluten-free.** One example is shaped breads (such as braided challah). Since gluten-free bread dough will tend to be rather sticky and shapeless, you're better off using shaped pans vs. trying to mold the dough into anything other than a basic round or flatbread. That said, it IS possible—I've seen it done, just not by me!

❖ To lighten up baked items, replace some of the liquid in the recipe with **sparkling water**. This makes pancakes and breads fluffier.

❖ **Gluten-free baked items may not always brown the same way.** Check the item for doneness, rather than relying on color alone. If you like a deeper browned look on breads, you may want to sprinkle with cinnamon or paprika before baking.

...plus a few more reminders for gluten-free baking:

➢ **GLUTEN IS A BINDING INGREDIENT.** Therefore, you will need another binding ingredient to take its place. As mentioned on the last page, gums are an option—I usually use xanthan gum sparingly.

➢ **Eggs help bind, too.** If a recipe calls for lots of eggs, you may not need additional binding ingredients—or you can always add a pinch of a gum to be sure.

➢ If your cake falls or your cookies spread, add more flour mix. Sometimes **GF recipes require a little extra "body" to bake correctly.**

MENU PLANNING

Before we go further, I think it's only fair that you understand the diet in our home. **We are almost completely vegetarian, dairy-free, and gluten-free.** Therefore, I will leave it up to you to add meats to your own menu; also, when I mention yogurt or cheese, in our home that means almond, coconut, or soy yogurt and rice or almond cheese. We also use margarine instead of butter (Miyoko's and Earth Balance are my usual picks).

On the next few pages I will share some of our favorite gluten-free meals. I think many of them would translate well to meat substitution if that is your preference. Do know that some celiac disease patients show a dairy/lactose intolerance after the diagnosis, at least until the intestine heals (and sometimes thereafter as well). Check with your medical practitioner about this if you suspect any ill effects from dairy in your child so that he/she can guide you accordingly.

Finally, if you are interested in recipes for these and other dishes, feel free to write to the Gluten-Free Parent directly (contact via glutenfreeparent.com).

ADAPTING MENUS FOR ENTERTAINING

As you look through the menus provided on these pages, consider the following general tips when adapting them for company, dinner parties, sleepovers, and other in-home entertaining:

- ✓ **Children—and people in general, when it comes to food—love to make-their-own anything**. Unless the event is very formal (as in a fancy dinner party, which for us is a few times a year), your guests will appreciate the opportunity to customize meals in a buffet-type setting. This works well with gluten-free, as you can focus on ingredients and create a feeling of bounty just by providing a fun selection of choices

- ✓ The truth is, **most people won't even notice that you are serving gluten-free** unless you tell them! We've done breakfasts after sleepovers, study lunches, dinners, and many a party without a mention of gluten-free. In fact, on many occasions it's been another friend's allergy that has altered the menu most!

Gluten-Free Family Favorites

Most of the below dishes are "regulars" in our home, which means we'll have them at least once or twice a month. I've also provided loose directions for each one. Try your own versions and collect your own favorites. Before long, you will realize that very little has changed in regard to the care and feeding of a healthy family!

- ❖ **Taco Bar:** Corn tortillas, seasoned beans and tofu (substitute chicken or beef if desired; we use GF taco seasoning mixes), chopped lettuce, tomato, avocado, cilantro, and cheese. I sometimes make refried beans by heating pinto beans with a little margarine and almond milk, then mashing. The kids love this meal!

- ❖ **"Kitchen Sink" Vegetable and Lentil Soup:** I chop up whatever veggies we have in the fridge—often including potatoes, celery, onion, and carrots—add a cup of lentils, and cover everything with water plus an extra 2-3" or so in the pot. Add GF bouillon and your seasonings of choice, then bring to a boil. Turn down temp to "low," place a pot on the soup, and let it simmer for a couple hours. Voila!

- ❖ **Coconut Milk Stir Fry:** This is another "kitchen sink" sort of recipe. In short, just sauté a selection of veggies. Add baked or pan-fried tofu or chicken, a can of coconut milk, and tamari sauce (or GF soy sauce) to taste. If you prefer a sweet/spicy version, add a teaspoon of ginger (or chopped fresh ginger) and a couple tablespoons of sugar or honey.

- ❖ **Make-Your-Own-Pizza:** We either buy the crusts ready-made, or mix up the dough (we like Outside the Breadbox ready-made crusts and Pamela's Pizza Crust Mix). Gather lots of fun toppings and a gluten-free sauce—and make your own masterpiece pizzas! The kids love this activity, especially when they have friends over for movies or slumber parties.

- ❖ **Pasta with "Meat" Sauce and Pesto:** We enjoy this meal every week, on average. Just sauté an onion and some garlic and add your favorite GF pasta sauce. We love Del Grosso Marinara. Then add GF veggie "meat" crumbles or pre-cooked meat. I make homemade basil pesto to serve as a side—just basil, garlic, nutritional yeast, salt, cashews or walnuts, and olive oil lightly blended in a food processor. Simply delicious!

- ❖ **Peanut Rice Noodles with Tofu (or chicken):** This is another simple one—just heat up ½ cup of peanut butter, and add tamari, sugar or honey, a splash of milk, and a bit of cornstarch for thickening. Add ginger to taste. Serve with rice noodles and cubed tofu or chicken for a protein-rich, yummy dish. Edyth likes hers topped with sliced sugar-snap peas, too.

❖ **Salad Bar Night:** This is no ordinary salad night…it's an everything-goes kind of salad spread. We've included hard-boiled eggs, shredded chicken (for the meat-eaters), olives, roasted veggies, and everything else you might put in a salad. You can make a homemade gluten-free dressing or buy one (so many options available!), and let everyone play artist and salad connoisseur for dinner.

❖ **Enchilada "Lasagna" Casserole:** This easy-breezy version of enchiladas as bursting with flavor and gluten-free goodness. Just layer enchilada sauce on the bottom of the pan, then follow with corn tortillas, beans, cheese, meats (if desired), tomatoes, salsa, and then the same order for another layer. Top with more corn tortillas, sauce, and cheese; bake in a moderate oven for an hour or until bubbly.

❖ **Barbecue Picnic Night:** When my husband and son want their red-meat fix, they turn on the grill and mix up some low-fat burgers to barbecue. Since we have one part of the grill reserved for veggie/gluten-free, that's when we break out the GF burgers or make our own sloppy joes out of veggie crumbles and seasonings. To go with the theme, we sometimes make a vegan potato salad (using Vegenaise) or French fries, baked beans (out of a can—sorry so lazy!), and serve with fresh lettuce and tomato. With a slightly junk-food-y meal like this, I often add healthy fruit smoothies full of antioxidants! Now, that's rationalization…

❖ **Rice-Stuffed Squash:** This dish looks quite festive and is great for a more formal dinner party setting, even though it also translates well to an ordinary night at home. Just cook brown and/or wild rice according to package directions, adding soup seasoning to the water. Once cooked, add sautéed vegetables of your choice—we like onions, mushrooms, garlic, and asparagus—but anything you choose will be delicious. Blend all together, season further if desired, and place inside of baked and halved acorn squash. Warm again with a sprinkling of mozzarella or pine nuts on top; serve with a parsley or rosemary garnish.

❖ **Savory Potato Stew:** I make this in a Pyrex casserole dish with a top—so easy! Just cube red, white, or baby potatoes (sized as you wish) and pour in just enough water to cover them. Add a can of fire-roasted tomatoes, chopped onions, and add any additional veggies your family likes: chopped carrots, zucchini, broccoli, mushrooms, etc.), along with GF soup cubes and seasonings. I also add ½ cup of cashews for extra protein. Bake at 350 degrees with the top on the dish; check after 1 hour. This dish may take closer to 1.5 – 2 hours, depending on vegetables.

❖ **More Ideas:** BLT sandwiches with tomato soup (we make GF coconut "bacon"—yum!), baked potato bar with broccoli and gravy, squash soup, corn chowder, sesame tofu (or chicken), GF Shepard's pie, chili with cornbread, "Breakfast for Dinner" complete with berry pancakes, salad, and homemade orange smoothies, and whatever new recipe just begs to be tried. Not many limitations, right?

School Lunch Ideas

When it comes to school lunches, variety is key. **Kids love to have options**, including colors, textures, and flavors—and maybe even something to share. Edyth never complained about having to take her lunch; I don't know if this was just luck, or if it had to do with the fun new lunchboxes she got to pick out each year (we always donated the old ones, by the way). In any case, all you need is a good ice-pack and some of these items at the ready for your child to grab and go:

➢ **Yogurt and granola with fruit**

➢ **Corn tortillas (or other GF versions) for wrapping peanut butter, salad fixings, meats/tofu, and/or cheeses**

➢ **The good old standby PBJ on gluten-free bread or rolls**

➢ **Hummus with vegetables and crackers**

➢ **Oatmeal with berries (either leftover mixed with extra milk, or dry if hot water is available)**

➢ **Cheese sticks with nut crackers and a fresh orange**

➢ **Sliced apples with nut butter, cubed hard cheese, or honey for dipping**

➢ **Celery with cottage cheese or nut butter**

➢ **Cold gf pizza (leftover or make ahead); Edyth loves it with pineapple and jalapeño or black olives and spinach**

➢ **Hard-boiled eggs with mustard or mayo and chopped celery (your child can make his own egg salad at school), or made-ahead salad**

➢ **Cold potato salad**

➢ **Peanut noodles with sugar snap peas**

➢ **Tuna salad with chopped apples and celery**

➢ **Pesto pasta with grape tomatoes (you can add cold chicken, tofu, and/or nuts for more protein)**

➢ **Gluten-free bagels with your spread of choice and fruit**

➢ **Chilled quinoa salad with corn, scallions, and almonds (parmesan optional)**

Edyth's World-Famous Gluten-Free and Vegan (optional)
Chocolate Chip Cookies

Drum roll, please….These are the best chocolate chip cookies in the whole gluten-free world! A secret no more, these have left many a hungry snacker absolutely stumped and in disbelief that they are actually GLUTEN-FREE. I've provided the vegan version, which includes our "vegan egg" recipe as well. Please keep in mind that the vegan egg in this recipe is especially formulated for use in crispy baked goods; it is not meant to be used as a substitute for egg dishes or eggs in casseroles or meringues.

Ingredients and Directions:

- ½ c margarine (we like Earth Balance whipped)
- ½ c brown sugar, packed
- ¼ c granulated sugar
- 1 chia egg (you may use a regular egg if desired)

> *Chia egg recipe: Mix 1 T chia seeds with 4 T warm water,*
> *½ t baking soda, and 1 t vanilla. Let sit for 10 minutes before using.*

Mix together until well-blended. Then add:

- 1 ¼ c flour mix
- ½ c almond flour
- ¼ c oatmeal

Mix again to blend before adding:

- ½ c chocolate chips
- ½ c walnuts (optional)

Fold together all ingredients until chips and nuts are evenly dispersed. Chill in refrigerator for an hour for best results. Then drop on cookie sheet and baked at 355 degrees for around 10 minutes. Watch cookies closely after 7 minutes, as baking times may vary due to the oven or the climate. Remove when browned; cool and enjoy!

Now it's Up to YOU:
Resources to help you continue in your gluten-free parenting evolution

For Medical Expertise and Information:
Celiac Disease Foundation: celiac.org
National Celiac Association: nationalceliac.org
Children's National: childrensnational.org
Colorado Center for Celiac Disease: childrenscolorado.org

A Few Excellent International Sites:
Canadian Celiac Association: celiac.ca
Coeliac New Zealand: coeliac.org.nz
Association of European Coeliac Societies: aoecs.org

Our Go-To All-Purpose Sites (each has special pages for kids):
Gluten-Free Living: glutenfreeliving.com
Gluten Intolerance Group of North America: gluten.org
GIG for kids: gluten.org/kids/
Beyond Celiac: beyondceliac.org
Beyond Celiac Kids Central: beyondceliac.org/living-with-celiac-disease/kids

Our Favorite Recipe/Lifestyle Sites:
glutenbee.com
glutenfreemom.com
glutenfreeforgood.com/blog
lifeglutenfree.com
Gluten Free Living and Recipe Share (Facebook group)
fearlessdining.com
simplysugarandglutenfree.com *(sugar and gluten-free)*
againstallgrain.com *(grain, gluten, and dairy-free)*
forkandbeans.com *(egg-free, dairy-free, and gluten-free)*
poorandglutenfree.blogspot.ca *(gluten-free on a budget)*

Gluten-Free Candy Reference:
celiac.org/gluten-free-living/gluten-free-foods/gluten-free-candy-list

Gluten-Free Medication Reference:
glutenfreedrugs.com

Helpful Apps (for iPhone):
findmeglutenfree
allergyeats
The Gluten-Free Scanner

Recommended Supplemental Books:
Mayo Clinic Going Gluten-Free: Essential Guide to Managing Celiac Disease and Related Conditions by Joseph A. Murray, M.D. (2014)
Gluten Free Buyers Guide: 2019 by Josh Schieffer, CSP
Gluten-Free Diet: A Comprehensive Resource Guide by Shelley Case (2010)
Gluten Freedom by Alessio Fasano, M.D. (2014)

Books Especially for Kids:
Dear Celiac by Kristen Adam (2019)
Gluten-Free is Part of Me by Laurie Oestreich (2018)
Mommy, What is Celiac Disease? A look at the sunny side of being a gluten-free kid by Katie Chalmers (2010)
201 Gluten-Free Recipes for Kids by Carrie S. Forbes (2013)

Gluten-Free Periodicals:
Gluten-Free Living
Simply Gluten Free Magazine
Delight Gluten-Free Magazine

Gluten-Free Camps—some feature one-week GF sessions; others are solely GF:
Camp Celiac/Livermore, California: celiaccamp.com

Camp Weekaneatit/Warm Springs, Georgia: glutenfreecamp.org

Gluten-Free Fun Camp/Maple Lake, Minnesota: twincitiesrock.org

Camp Emerson/Hinsdale, Massachusetts: campemerson.com

Camp Eagle Hill/Elizaville, New York: campeaglehill.com

Gluten-Free Week at Camp Kanata/Wake Forest, North Carolina: campkanata.org

Gluten Intolerance Camp at Camp Sealth/Vashon Island, Washington: campfireseattle.org

Camp Celiac/North Scituate, Rhode Island: campceliac.org

Celiac Disease Foundation's Campership Program scholarship opportunities: celiac.org/camp
*(camp list compiled by **glutenfreeliving.com**)*

...and indeed,

as I mentioned at the start...

everything

—yet nothing—

has changed.

About the Author

*Elyn Joy, "The Gluten-Free Parent," is a Denver-based author, career educator, and mom of two thriving young-adult children—one of whom has gone through many stages and phases of a gluten-free childhood. Elyn's optimistic wisdom on gluten-free parenting has helped countless parents and organizations through the years. Her writings and advice have been featured in **Gluten-Free Living** and **Allergic Living** (interview), as well as in other celiac education and lifestyle venues. Beyond her Gluten-Free Parenting projects, Elyn has written extensively in the education world, including two beloved children's books: **Everyone has a Point of View** (2018) and **Once Upon a Pigeon and Other Retold Fables** (CR Success Learning, 2019). She lives in a "vine-covered storybook house" (her daughter's words) in Colorado, USA, with her husband, almost-grown children, and two silly cats.*

With Special Thanks to...

Gregory Ross

Edyth and Oliver

Dr. Raymond Moldow

Lisa Logan

Natural Grocers Stores

Dr. Ed Hoffenberg and

The Colorado Center for Celiac Disease

Dr. Erika Moldow

Debi Mira and Eliot Ray

Samuel and Dorothy Shindler

...and all our family, friends, teachers, and healthcare professionals for their ongoing support.

glutenfreeparent.com / Denver, Colorado USA

Made in the USA
San Bernardino,
CA